ATTACK ON CIRCUIT CITY

Catherine Casey

Quarto is the authority on a wide range of topics.

Quarto educates, entertains and enriches the lives of our readers—enthusiasts and lovers of hands-on living.

www.quartoknows.com

Author: Catherine Casey
Illustrator: Cory Godbey
Consultants: Hilary Koll & Steve Mills
Editor: Amanda Askew
Designer: Punch Bowl Design
QED Editor: Carly Madden

First published in the UK in 2017 by
QED Publishing
Part of The Quarto Group
The Old Brewery
6 Blundell Street
London, N7 9BH

A catalogue record for this book is available from the British Library.

ISBN 978-1-78493-853-6

Printed in China

MIX
Paper from responsible sources
FSC® C016973
www.fsc.org

HOW TO BEGIN YOUR ADVENTURE

Are you ready for a brain-bending mission packed with puzzles and problems?

Then this is the book for you!

Attack on Circuit City isn't like other books where you read through the pages in order. It's a lot more exciting than that because you're the main person in the story! You have to find your own way through the book, flicking backwards and forwards, following the clues until you've finished the whole adventure.

The story starts on page 4, and then tells you where to go next. Every time you face a challenge, you'll have a choice of answers, which look something like this:

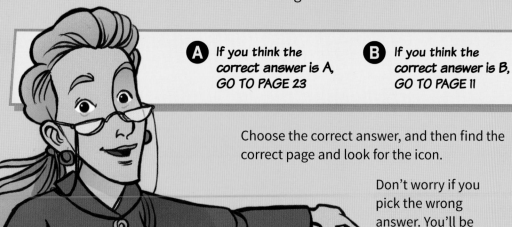

A If you think the correct answer is A, GO TO PAGE 23

B If you think the correct answer is B, GO TO PAGE 11

Choose the correct answer, and then find the correct page and look for the icon.

Don't worry if you pick the wrong answer. You'll be given an extra clue, then you can go back and try again.

The puzzles and problems in *Attack on Circuit City* are all about the super world of statistics, so have your maths skills ready!

To help you there's a list of useful words at the back of the book, starting on page 44.

Are you ready?

Then turn the page and let's get started!

ATTACK ON CIRCUIT CITY

It's a quiet afternoon in the library and you're finishing your maths homework. When you try to save your work, a beetle appears on your screen.

REQUEST FOR UPDATE GRANTED.
VIRUSES TO
"**DESTROY** CIRCUIT CITY"
ARE 57% UPLOADED.
COMPLETION IN 2 HOURS.

Circuit City is the nickname for the school's **network** of computers – why would anyone want to destroy that? You're going to find out!

 There's no time to lose!
START YOUR QUEST ON PAGE 31.

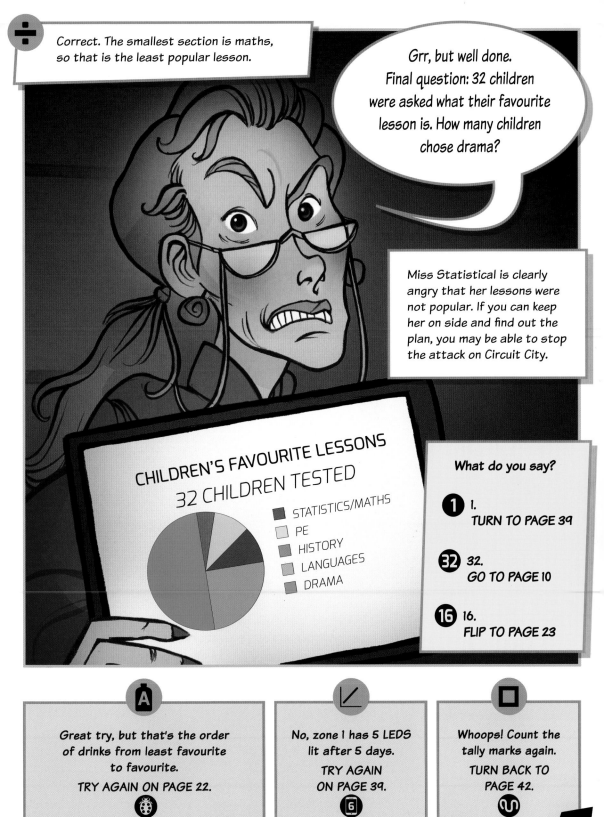

Correct! 66 children attended after-school clubs. The door opens and you step through just in time!

You wait for the Beetle to pass and look out of the door...

You hear more feet coming!

More Beetles! Miss Statistical must have already activated the Beetle virus and it's **multiplying** on a loop.

You check your watch. It's been 30 minutes since the virus was activated. How many Beetles are there now?

2:20 PM

You sketch a line graph to help you work it out.

How quickly the Beetles are multiplying

Number of Beetles

80
70
60
50
40
30
20
10

5 10 15 20 25 30 35 40 45 50 55 60

Minutes

How many Beetles are there?

30 beetles.
TURN TO PAGE 8

15 beetles.
GO TO PAGE 18

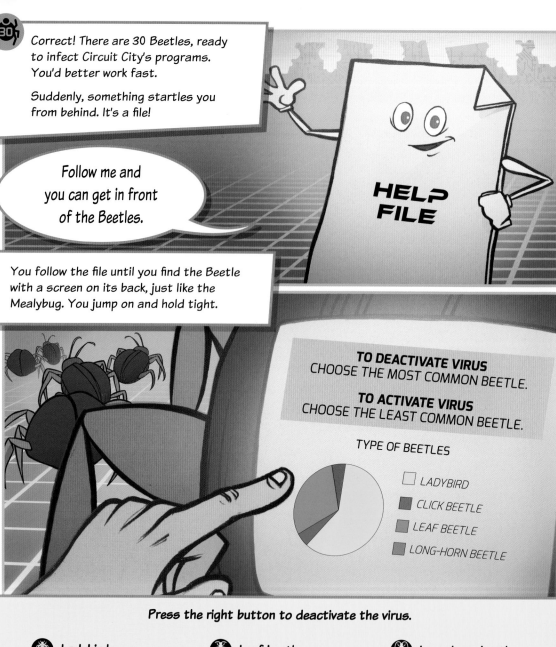

Correct! There are 30 Beetles, ready to infect Circuit City's programs. You'd better work fast.

Suddenly, something startles you from behind. It's a file!

Follow me and you can get in front of the Beetles.

You follow the file until you find the Beetle with a screen on its back, just like the Mealybug. You jump on and hold tight.

HELP FILE

TO DEACTIVATE VIRUS
CHOOSE THE MOST COMMON BEETLE.

TO ACTIVATE VIRUS
CHOOSE THE LEAST COMMON BEETLE.

TYPE OF BEETLES

☐ LADYBIRD
◼ CLICK BEETLE
◼ LEAF BEETLE
◼ LONG-HORN BEETLE

Press the right button to deactivate the virus.

 Ladybird.
WHIZZ TO PAGE 22

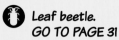 Leaf beetle.
GO TO PAGE 31

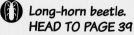 Long-horn beetle.
HEAD TO PAGE 39

Try again. The science lab has the highest internet usage. Remember to use the key next to the graph.
BACK TO PAGE 19 FOR ANOTHER GO.

16

Password rejected. Remember the 5th mark goes across the previous 4. Practise counting in 5s.
TRY AGAIN ON PAGE 33.

15

Super work! You reset the position of the wasp's stinger and it starts to repair the wires.

All bugs have been deactivated. Fantastic! Then you hear Sam's booming voice again.

Traitor! I've damaged the network card so you can't leave through the same portal! Ha! But, I'm fair, so I'll help you find a way out, if you can answer this tricky question.

PREFERRED USE OF TECHNOLOGY FOR INTERNET RESEARCH

NUMBER OF CHILDREN

TYPE OF TECHNOLOGY

He sends you a graph and asks: How many more children preferred to use a mobile phone than a laptop computer?

 6.
GO TO PAGE 39

 11.
TURN TO PAGE 23

Incorrect. The line graph shows how many files will be destroyed over time. Find 10 minutes along the x-axis and read across to the y-axis to find the answer.
TURN BACK TO PAGE 38 TO TRY AGAIN.

No, the upload started at 11:00 am.
TAKE A CLOSER LOOK ON PAGE 23.
16

Correct! He's put the portal in zone 3 – the zone you're in! Be quick, before Miss Statistical beats you to it and closes the portal.

Miss Statistical runs one way and you try the other way. You find the portal door, but it keeps moving away from you.

You have an idea that just might work.

Sam, let's have one final challenge. Ask me any question – if I win, you'll stop the portal from moving. If you win, I stay and play forever.

Sam can't resist and asks you a question that only students two years above can usually answer.

He asks: Which type of graph or chart shows how one **variable** changes as another changes?

 Line graph.
JUMP TO PAGE 33

 Bar chart.
WHIZZ TO PAGE 20

 Pie chart.
LEAP TO PAGE 36

32

Incorrect! 32 is the total number of children asked and half the children chose drama.
TRY AGAIN ON PAGE 5.

30

Try again! 30 is the median – the middle number of mealybugs.
QUICKLY PRESS THE RIGHT BUTTON ON PAGE 27 BEFORE IT'S TOO LATE.

Well done – there are only 8 worms! Sam reboots the short-term memory and disappears.

Time to get to zone 2 to find the Beetle virus. When you reach the edge of the circuit board, the bridges to the other zones have collapsed. Miss Statistical appears.

I've taken down the bridges because you're not following the plan! Answer a question correctly and I'll help you across, so you can watch the Beetle devour the RAM. How many maths tests will I set this year?

MATHS TESTS COMING UP THIS YEAR

AREA OF MATHEMATICS

ALGEBRA
MEASUREMENTS
GEOMETRY
STATISTICS
ARITHMETIC

1   2   3   4
NUMBER OF TESTS

She sends you a graph. What do you answer?

12 tests.
GO TO PAGE 20

24 tests.
JUMP TO PAGE 16

Well done – although you're going to zone 3 first, it's a shorter route.

You build both bridges and edge your way across.

TO FIND RAM, FOLLOW TRUE STATEMENT.
TO FIND CPU, FOLLOW FALSE STATEMENT.

33 PUPILS PLAY TENNIS ←

8 PUPILS PLAY HOCKEY →

SPORTS THAT PUPILS PLAY AT YOUR SCHOOL

TENNIS
RUGBY
FOOTBALL
HOCKEY
BASKETBALL

KEY: 1 PICTURE = 3 PUPILS

Miss Statistical said that the Beetle virus is in the RAM. You run ahead and reach a crossroads.

What direction do you go?

33 pupils play tennis.
TURN TO PAGE 18

8 pupils play hockey.
GO TO PAGE 37

55

Wrong answer! Add together the number of computer tablets and the number of laptops to find your answer.
TRY AGAIN ON PAGE 31.

△

No, you've misread the pie chart. Take another look and start with the biggest zone with the highest percentage.
TRY AGAIN ON PAGE 32.

You put in a video call to Sam – and he answers! You realize that it's an internal call and he's inside the school.

The game is up, Sam. We just need to get Miss Statistical out safely. Can we work together to do that?

Together? I'm a genius and don't need anyone. I'll send you the latest Maths test results – can you see how much better I am?

STUDENT SCORES IN THE MATHS TESTS

CHILD

SAM
BETH
BEN
JAKE
ZOE

0   5   10   15   20   25   30
NUMBER OF POINTS

A

No, a frequency chart is a table with three columns – the options, a tally and a frequency total.

TURN BACK TO PAGE 29.

You nod enthusiastically. How many more points did Sam get than the next highest score?

30.
TURN TO PAGE 28

27.
GO TO PAGE 26

3.
WHIZZ TO PAGE 32

75
That's right! ¾ or 75% of the children have been stung by a wasp.
The Wasp starts zapping wildly – what's going on?
Sam's voice booms out.
Ha ha! We switched the programming of the wasp to stop you. By activating it a second time, you've doubled its destructive speed!

Oh no! He must've been watching you. You shout for help and a question mark appears.

Looks like you need to get off this wasp. Would you like some help?

You ask how to deactivate the wasp and the question mark presents you with instructions.

Work out the differences between the number of wasps and bees spotted on each day, add these 3 numbers together and enter the total into the virus's keypad.

WASPS AND BEES SPOTTED ON EACH DAY

NUMBER OF BUGS SPOTTED

DAY 1   DAY 2   DAY 3

KEY
BEES
WASPS

Which number do you enter?

4. TURN TO PAGE 21

3. JUMP TO PAGE 42

5. GO TO PAGE 37

That's right! 3 viruses have been uploaded. Sam just gives you a cold, hard stare.

We'll both enter the system. I'll start with the Beetle, you go to the Mealybug and whoever finishes first, can activate the Wasp. The viruses each have activation instructions.

ENTER CIRCUIT CITY

ARE YOU SURE YOU WANT TO UPLOAD YOURSELVES TO CIRCUIT CITY?

OK

It'll be scary, but you have the chance to shut down the viruses, so you agree.

As the computer's countdown reaches zero, there's a flash and you're both sucked inside the system.
GO TO PAGE 24.

24

That's not right. Check the x-axis and count carefully.
TRY AGAIN ON PAGE 11.

25

A good try, but remember that 25% is the same as ¼, so you need to work out ¼ of 60.
HAVE ANOTHER GO ON PAGE 37. 5

13 Correct! The mean number is 13 (19 + 11 + 9 = 39, and 39 ÷ 3 = 13).

You type 13 into the keypad and the Mealybug freezes. One virus down, two to go! Suddenly, a booming voice echoes around the whole system.

It's Sam and he's on to you!

I knew it! You're not a star pupil. No one can take that title away from me! But what will you do if the files think YOU are the virus? Ha ha!

All the surrounding files start to move towards you. You notice an instruction panel that will make the walkway they're on move!

TO MOVE WALKWAY BACKWARDS:
Press the number indicating how many more Mealybugs there are in zone 1 than zone 3.

TO MOVE WALKWAY FORWARDS:
Press the number indicating how many more Mealybugs there are in zone 2 than zone 3.

MEALYBUGS THAT WILL BE RELEASED AROUND CIRCUIT CITY

ZONE	TALLY	FREQUENCY
ZONE 1	||||| ||||| ||||| ||||	19
ZONE 2	||||| |||||		11
ZONE 3	||||| ||||	

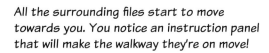

What number do you type in?

10.
TURN TO PAGE 28

28.
GO TO PAGE 30

2.
JUMP TO PAGE 42

That's right; 33 pupils play tennis – each picture stands for 3 pupils. You follow the arrow towards the RAM.

The Beetle virus, which is eating everything in its path, is coming towards you. You notice a door where you can escape, but you need to press a button to open it.

ENTER THE TOTAL NUMBER OF PUPILS ATTENDING AFTER-SCHOOL CLUBS.

PUPILS ATTENDING AFTER-SCHOOL CLUBS.

CHESS
MUSIC/CHOIR
DANCE
COOKERY
ART

KEY: 1 PICTURE = 2 PUPILS

69   33   66

Which button should you press to get out of the Beetle's way – and quickly?

 69. TURN TO PAGE 23

 33. GO TO PAGE 41

 66. FIND PAGE 6

No, to get 30 you must have missed out one of the zones.
TRY AGAIN ON PAGE 25.

Try again! Zone 2 has only 1 LED lit after 5 days.
HAVE ANOTHER GO ON PAGE 39.

No, there is more than that. Look carefully at the line graph and try again.
GO BACK TO PAGE 7.

Well done! The most popular area of maths is Measures with 12 children choosing this option.

You bring up a graph showing the school's computer activity this week. Whoever has been planning the attack will have spent hours programming the viruses.

THE SCHOOL'S COMPUTER ACTIVITY THIS WEEK

KEY
HOURS SPENT DOWNLOADING
HOURS SPENT ON INTERNET
HOURS SPENT PROGRAMMING

NUMBER OF HOURS

MATHS CLASSROOM
SCIENCE LAB
DRAMA STUDIO
ENGLISH DEPARTMENT
HISTORY CLASSROOM

Where have computers been used for programming the most?

Drama studio.
TURN TO PAGE 33

Maths classroom.
FLICK TO PAGE 29

Science lab.
GO TO PAGE 8

That's right – 12 tests.

You are not looking forward to that!

Miss Statistical reveals instructions that will get the bridges up again, then she disappears.

WIRES NEEDED TO BUILD BRIDGES

ZONE ROUTE	NUMBER OF WIRES
1 TO 2	
1 TO 3	✚✚✚✚✚ ✚✚✚✚✚
3 TO 2	IIII
	IIII

You study the instructions carefully. Time is running out!

You are in zone 1. Which route to zone 2 will take the fewest wires?

← Zone 1 to 2.
GO TO PAGE 38

→ Zone 1 to 3, then 3 to 2.
TURN TO PAGE 12

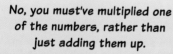

No, you must've multiplied one of the numbers, rather than just adding them up.

HAVE ANOTHER GO ON PAGE 25.

Oh dear! No, a bar chart shows bars of different lengths, each representing a different amount.

HAVE ANOTHER GO ON PAGE 10.

84

Correct – there are 84 tally marks.

You whirl through the portal and land in the maths classroom, back where you started.

Firstly, you tell Mr Graff, the headteacher, about the attack. With Miss Statistical inside Circuit City, the network is still in danger.

 Mr Graff phones for back-up while you use his computer to locate Sam ON PAGE 13.

A good try but 14 is the total number of viruses. Remember to use the key.

TURN BACK TO PAGE 36 AND HAVE ANOTHER GO.

4

No, 4 isn't the total of all the differences.

LOOK AT EACH SET OF BARS SEPARATELY AGAIN ON PAGE 15. **75**

Yes! The ladybird is the most common beetle.

You spot a file nearby saying 'SHORTCUT TO ZONE 3'. You open it.

SHORTCUT TO ZONE 3

Big mistake! The file wraps wire around you so you can't move. Suddenly Miss Statistical appears.

Ha! I see you've met the Trojan... the Mealybug and the Beetle are gone, but the Wasp will work!

She then disappears!

You know that every virus has an **anti-virus**, so you ask to see the Trojan's screen.

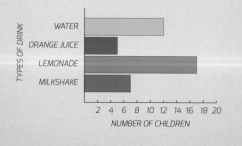

TO DEACTIVATE TROJAN
SAY ALOUD THE CHILDREN'S DRINKS FROM FAVOURITE TO LEAST FAVOURITE.

TO ACTIVATE TROJAN
SAY ALOUD THE CHILDREN'S DRINKS FROM LEAST FAVOURITE TO FAVOURITE.

TYPES OF DRINK
WATER
ORANGE JUICE
LEMONADE
MILKSHAKE

2 4 6 8 10 12 14 16 18 20
NUMBER OF CHILDREN

Take a look at the bar chart and very carefully say the right answer.

 A

Orange juice, milkshake, water, lemonade.
GO TO PAGE 5

 B

Lemonade, water, milkshake, orange juice.
TURN TO PAGE 43

 C

Water, milkshake, lemonade, orange juice.
FLIP TO PAGE 26

16

Correct! The pie chart shows that half the children chose drama and half of 32 is 16.

Miss Statistical asks you to look at her computer screen.

One chose maths!
Revenge time! By destroying Circuit City, the drama department's show will be cancelled. A maths competition can take its place.

TIMELINE OF UPLOADS

STAGE 0: *Preparation time*
STAGE 1: *Program bugs*
STAGE 2: *Upload bug one*
STAGE 3: *Upload bug two*
STAGE 4: *Upload bug three*
STAGE 5: *Check bug uploads are successful*
STAGE 6: **Activate** *bugs*

TIME IN HOURS

You decide to play along so that you can find out more information. Miss Statistical smiles at your enthusiasm and shows you her timeline.

What time will the uploads be completed?

 11:00 a.m.
JUMP TO PAGE 9

 3:00 p.m.
GO TO PAGE 36

 11:30 a.m.
FLIP TO PAGE 30

Incorrect – remember each picture represents 2 pupils.
TRY AGAIN ON PAGE 18 BEFORE YOU ARE EATEN!

11

Almost – that's the total number of children who chose the mobile phone option. You need to find the difference between that and the laptop option.
TRY AGAIN ON PAGE 9. **15**

You land with a thump. Surrounding you is a giant maze of circuit boards, memory chips and wires with files, programs and codes zooming about. It's just like a city – this is why it's nicknamed Circuit City!

As your eyes focus again, you watch Miss Statistical disappear. You make your way down a path on the circuit board. From nowhere, the Mealybug appears – the first virus!

Hello, Mealybug. I'm here to activate you. First, show me your destruction program.

A table appears on the Mealybug's screen. It shows the zones of Circuit City and the number of Mealybugs that will be released in each.

MEALYBUGS THAT WILL BE RELEASED AROUND CIRCUIT CITY

ZONE	TALLY	FREQUENCY
ZONE 1	ЖЖ ЖЖ ЖЖ IIII	19
ZONE 2	ЖЖ ЖЖ I	11
ZONE 3	ЖЖ IIII	

How many Mealybugs will be released in total?

39.
GO TO PAGE 38

30.
FLIP TO PAGE 18

270.
TURN TO PAGE 20

Fantastic! You read the **bar chart** correctly. There are 35 computer tablets and 25 laptops – a total of 60.

You unlock the door and find the Control Computer. You wiggle the mouse and the screen asks for a password.

```
CONTROL COMPUTER LOG-IN
        ENTER PASSWORD
┌─────────────────────────┐
│                         │
└─────────────────────────┘
    CLUE: THE MOST POPULAR
        MATHS SUBJECT.
```

You look around the room and spot a **frequency chart**. You smile – the teachers set such easy passwords!

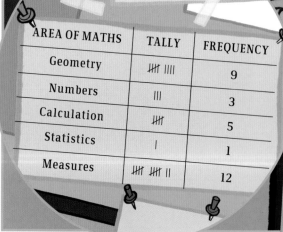

AREA OF MATHS	TALLY	FREQUENCY
Geometry	IIII IIII	9
Numbers	III	3
Calculation	IIII	5
Statistics	I	1
Measures	IIII IIII II	12

What is the password?

Measures.
GO TO PAGE 19

Geometry.
TURN TO PAGE 37

Try again! Although you may like water, it's not the favourite drink of the children asked.

HAVE ANOTHER LOOK AT THE CHART ON PAGE 22.

Incorrect! 27 is the score that Jake earned – he is the second highest scorer.

USE THIS INFORMATION TO HELP YOU ANSWER AGAIN ON PAGE 13.

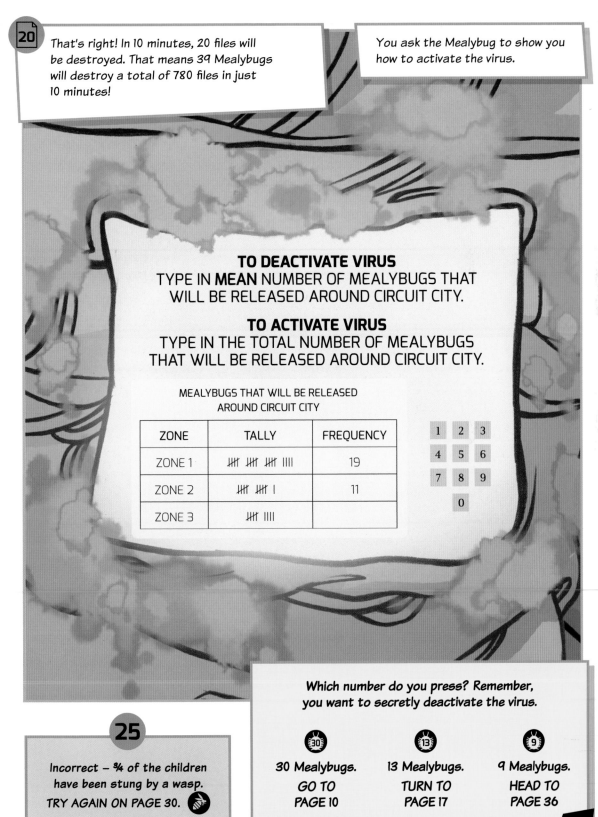

20

That's right! In 10 minutes, 20 files will be destroyed. That means 39 Mealybugs will destroy a total of 780 files in just 10 minutes!

You ask the Mealybug to show you how to activate the virus.

TO DEACTIVATE VIRUS
TYPE IN **MEAN** NUMBER OF MEALYBUGS THAT WILL BE RELEASED AROUND CIRCUIT CITY.

TO ACTIVATE VIRUS
TYPE IN THE TOTAL NUMBER OF MEALYBUGS THAT WILL BE RELEASED AROUND CIRCUIT CITY.

MEALYBUGS THAT WILL BE RELEASED
AROUND CIRCUIT CITY

ZONE	TALLY	FREQUENCY
ZONE 1	ⅢⅢ ⅢⅢ ⅢⅢ IIII	19
ZONE 2	ⅢⅢ ⅢⅢ I	11
ZONE 3	ⅢⅢ IIII	

1	2	3
4	5	6
7	8	9
	0	

25

Incorrect – ¾ of the children have been stung by a wasp.
TRY AGAIN ON PAGE 30.

Which number do you press? Remember, you want to secretly deactivate the virus.

30
30 Mealybugs.
GO TO
PAGE 10

13
13 Mealybugs.
TURN TO
PAGE 17

9
9 Mealybugs.
HEAD TO
PAGE 36

Correct! There were 10 more mealybugs in zone 1 – the difference between 19 and 9. The walkway moves the files away from you. Time to get going!

NUMBER OF BUGS FOUND IN THE SCHOOL GARDEN

LADYBIRDS BEETLES SNAILS WORMS ANTS

KEY: 1 PICTURE = 2 BUGS

Lucky escape. But now I've deactivated the short-term memory. Do you want to answer a question to reboot it?

You have no choice but to answer the question. BEEP BEEP! Sam has sent you a **pictogram**.

He asks: Which bug is the least **common**?

 Beetles.
TURN TO PAGE 33

 Worms.
FLICK TO PAGE 11

 Whoops! Drama is the MOST popular with 50% choosing this option – that's half the children asked.
LOOK AGAIN AT THE CHART ON PAGE 41 TO FIND THE LEAST POPULAR. **B**

 No, 30 is the score that Sam achieved.
TAKE ANOTHER LOOK ON PAGE 13.

Well done. The maths classroom computer has been programming for hours. It must be the host!

You run to the maths classroom. The lights are off, but the door is half open, so you go in. Suddenly, you sense you're not alone – Miss Statistical, the maths teacher, is in the shadows.

I know you've released viruses to attack Circuit City. Why?

CHILDREN'S FAVOURITE LESSONS
32 CHILDREN TESTED

- STATISTICS/MATHS
- PE
- HISTORY
- LANGUAGES
- DRAMA

Hmmm, you've always been a good student. If you can answer three tricky questions, I'll let you in on my plan. Question one: What type of chart is this?

What do you say?

A Frequency chart.
TURN TO PAGE 13

B Pie chart.
LEAP TO PAGE 41

At the very last minute, you dodge out of the way and jump on its back. The Wasp somersaults to try to throw you off.

I'm doing such a good job; you won't stop me!

TO DEACTIVATE VIRUS, SAY ALOUD HOW MANY CHILDREN HAVE BEEN STUNG BY A WASP.
TO ACTIVATE VIRUS, SAY ALOUD HOW MANY CHILDREN HAVEN'T BEEN STUNG BY A WASP.

CHILDREN WHO HAVE BEEN STUNG BY A WASP

☐ YES
■ NO

With one hand holding on tightly, you locate the instruction panel.

The wasp is spinning now. What you say?

 25% of children have been stung by a wasp.
FLIP TO PAGE 27

 75% of children have been stung by a wasp.
GO TO PAGE 14

28

Not quite – you have found the total number of bugs in zones 1 and 3 together (19 + 9 = 28). You need to find the difference.
TRY AGAIN ON PAGE 17.

No, bug 2 will start uploading at 11:30 a.m.
LOOK AGAIN ON PAGE 23.

You decide to find the host computer, starting with the Control Computer in the ICT room, but the door is locked. You notice a key safe and a clue to open it!

Code = number of computer tablets + number of laptops

What number do you type in?

55.
TURN TO PAGE 12

60.
GO TO PAGE 26

45.
JUMP TO PAGE 42

 Try again! Although 30% is quite a lot, it isn't the most common beetle.
HAVE ANOTHER GO ON PAGE 8.

 Incorrect. Check the scale on the y-axis carefully.
TRY AGAIN ON PAGE 40.

Correct! Sam scored 3 points more than the next highest mark by Jake (30 − 27 = 3).

You hear a victorious yell... coming from the cupboard. When you open the door, Sam touches his screen and is sucked into his tablet. You need to get them both out!

Mr Graff, I could try shutting down all zones to trap them. Then program a portal to bring them back. What do you think?

He nods. You click on the zones shutdown button and a list of instructions appears.

ZONES SHUTDOWN

TO SHUT DOWN ALL ZONES, PRESS ZONES IN THE ORDER OF SIZE, FROM BIGGEST TO SMALLEST.

ZONE 1
ZONE 2
ZONE 3

Which order do you choose?

▲

Zone 1, Zone 3, Zone 2.
TURN TO PAGE 12

◆

Zone 3, Zone 1, Zone 2.
GO TO PAGE 40

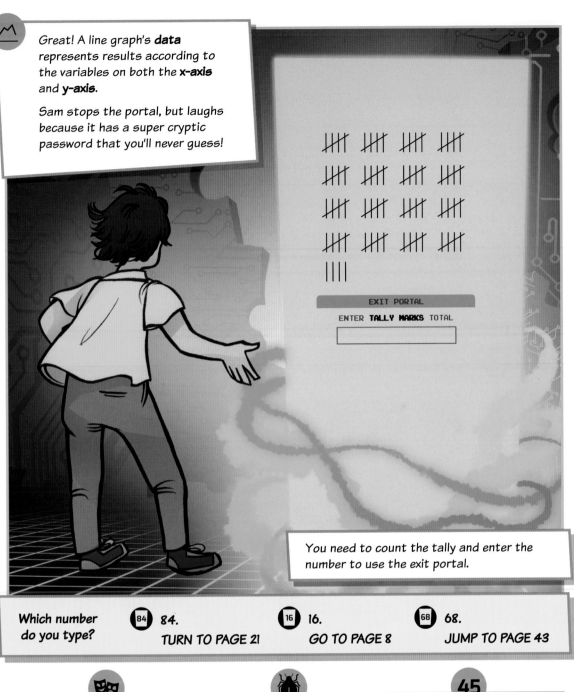

Great! A line graph's **data** represents results according to the variables on both the **x-axis** and **y-axis**.

Sam stops the portal, but laughs because it has a super cryptic password that you'll never guess!

~~HH~~ ~~HH~~ ~~HH~~ ~~HH~~
~~HH~~ ~~HH~~ ~~HH~~ ~~HH~~
~~HH~~ ~~HH~~ ~~HH~~ ~~HH~~
~~HH~~ ~~HH~~ ~~HH~~ ~~HH~~
IIII

EXIT PORTAL
ENTER **TALLY MARKS** TOTAL

You need to count the tally and enter the number to use the exit portal.

Which number do you type?

84 84.
TURN TO PAGE 21

16 16.
GO TO PAGE 8

68 68.
JUMP TO PAGE 43

That's not right. The drama studio has downloaded the most data, but they haven't been programming.
BACK TO PAGE 19 FOR ANOTHER GO.

No! The least common is the smallest amount.
TRY AGAIN ON PAGE 28.

45

Nearly! But 45 is the number of children that have been stung. You need to work out how many have not been stung.
TURN BACK TO PAGE 37.

5

Correct! You open File D, drop the portal next to Miss Statistical and Sam, and they step into it.

FLASH!

Miss Statistical and Sam come flying out of the maths computer, just as the Computer Corruption Team burst through the classroom door.

Before they have a chance to escape, they're handcuffed and taken away for questioning.

Excellent! The uploads will be completed at 3:00 p.m.

Only 2 hours to save Circuit City!

Miss Statistical answers a video call. Another student called Sam appears on the screen and asks why you're there.

She explains to Sam that you are on their side. In fact, you can help activate the viruses since Sam's arm is broken.

NUMBER OF VIRUSES UPLOADED

Mealybug					
Beetle					
Wasp					
Trojan					
Worms					

KEY

1 picture = 1 virus

■ uploaded ■ not uploaded

Sam eyes you suspiciously and challenges you to work out how many viruses have been uploaded.

How many viruses have been uploaded?

14. HEAD TO PAGE 21

11. GO TO PAGE 43

3. JUMP TO PAGE 16

Incorrect. To calculate the mean you need to add up the number of mealybugs and divide by the number of zones.
TRY AGAIN ON PAGE 27.

Try again! A pie chart shows data in a circle that is divided into sections.
GO BACK TO PAGE 10 FOR ANOTHER TRY.

5 Right! The number you needed was 3 + 1 + 1 = 5. The Wasp calmly lands and lets you off its back.

Thank you. The virus programming took over my brain. Oh, what have I done! The wires are ruined.

Perhaps you can be reprogrammed to fuse the wires together.

TO REVERSE THE DAMAGE, RESET THE STINGER TO THE NUMBER OF CHILDREN NOT STUNG.

60 CHILDREN QUESTIONED ABOUT WHETHER THEY HAVE BEEN STUNG

STUNG
NOT STUNG

You ask the question mark if this is possible and it shows you a way!

Out of the 60 children asked if they had been stung, how many children had not been stung?

25
25.
TURN TO PAGE 16

15
15.
GO TO PAGE 9

45
45.
JUMP TO PAGE 33

Incorrect! Remember, the most popular means the subject with the greatest number or highest frequency.
TURN BACK TO PAGE 26.

Whoops! You have forgotten to use the key – each picture represents 3 pupils!
TURN BACK TO PAGE 12 BEFORE YOU END UP AT THE CPU.

That's right! 39 Mealybugs will be released around Circuit City.

Next, you ask the Mealybug to show you how many files each virus can destroy. A **line graph** appears on the Mealybug's screen.

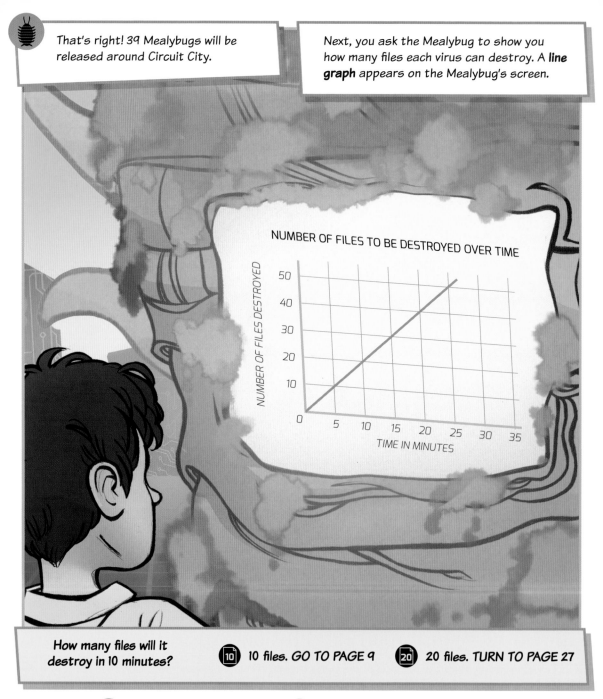

NUMBER OF FILES TO BE DESTROYED OVER TIME

NUMBER OF FILES DESTROYED

TIME IN MINUTES

How many files will it destroy in 10 minutes?

 10 files. GO TO PAGE 9

 20 files. TURN TO PAGE 27

No! There's a shorter bridge.
TRY AGAIN ON PAGE 20.

Oh dear! Look carefully at the bar chart.
HAVE ANOTHER TRY ON PAGE 40. ◆

No, you haven't counted correctly.
TRY AGAIN ON PAGE 42.

6 That's right, 11 − 5 = 6.

Sam shrieks in annoyance. Suddenly, Miss Statistical appears and yells – at Sam!

Sam, you may have stopped our traitor from leaving Circuit City, but you have also stopped me!

EMERGENCY PORTAL CAN BE FOUND IN THE ZONE WITH 3 LEDS LIT AFTER 5 DAYS.

Sam apologizes and says he's opened the emergency portal in the zone indicated by a chart that he sends you.

Which zone should you head for?

Zone 1.
GO TO PAGE 5

Zone 2.
TURN TO PAGE 18

Zone 3.
FLIP TO PAGE 10

1

Whoops. Drama was the most popular lesson with half of the children choosing it.
TURN BACK TO PAGE 5.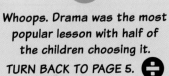

Incorrect! The pie chart shows four beetles. The most common beetle is the biggest section of the pie chart.
TURN TO PAGE 8 TO TRY AGAIN.

Correct, Zone 3 is the biggest.

The zones shut down and Miss Statistical and Sam are plunged into darkness. Sam is screaming for help. You ask what's wrong.

I released the worm viruses, but they've **malfunctioned** and they're attacking us. Look at my notebook for the anti-virus code. Please!

Mr Graff grabs the notebook from the cupboard and finds the anti-virus page.

worm anti-virus code:
Number of children in Miss Statistical's Year 6 maths group.

Number of pupils in each maths class

number of pupils

35
30
25
20
15
10
5
0

Year 5   Year 6   Year 7   Year 8

Which code do you tell Sam?

30.
GO TO PAGE 31

31.
JUMP TO PAGE 38

32.
TURN TO PAGE 42

B Well done! A pie chart is a circle divided into sections that each represent a proportion of the total.

Great, you listen in lessons! Second question: Which is the least popular lesson?

CHILDREN'S FAVOURITE LESSONS
32 CHILDREN TESTED

- STATISTICS/MATHS
- PE
- HISTORY
- LANGUAGES
- DRAMA

Study the chart carefully and give her your answer.

 Statistics/maths.
TURN TO PAGE 5

 Drama.
HEAD TO PAGE 28

 Whoops! Look closely at the numbers and the key.

TURN BACK TO PAGE 18 QUICKLY; THE BEETLE IS APPROACHING FAST.

Well done! You tell Sam the code and as he programs the anti-virus, the worms freeze.

Now you need to direct Miss Statistical and Sam to a portal. Which file contains a complete portal?

PORTAL FILES

FILE	TALLY
A	ⵏ⵱ ⵏ⵱ ⵏ⵱ ⵏ⵱ IIII
B	ⵏ⵱ ⵏ⵱ ⵏ⵱ ⵏ⵱ ⵏ⵱ ⵏ⵱ IIII
C	ⵏ⵱ ⵏ⵱ ⵏ⵱ ⵏ⵱ ⵏ⵱ I
D	ⵏ⵱ ⵏ⵱ ⵏ⵱ ⵏ⵱ ⵏ⵱
E	ⵏ⵱ ⵏ⵱ ⵏ⵱ ⵏ⵱ ⵏ⵱ ⵏ⵱ III

CLUE: 1 PORTAL = 25 STRIKES EXACTLY

Which file do you choose?

△ File A.
GO TO PAGE 38

● File D.
JUMP OVER TO PAGE 34

■ File B.
TURN TO PAGE 5

45
Whoops! The y-axis counts up in 5s.
TRY AGAIN ON PAGE 31.

2
No! 2 is the difference between the Mealybugs in zones 2 and 3 – and will move the bugs towards you!
HAVE ANOTHER TRY ON PAGE 17.

3
No, you've only looked at the first bars.
QUICKLY, THINK AGAIN ON PAGE 15.

B Correct! Most children liked lemonade the most and orange juice the least.

The file releases you and disappears.

You carry on around the circuit board until you reach zone 3, where you find disconnected wires.

You soon find out why – the Wasp virus has been activated and is destroying the connections and wires.

You need to get to the keypad. You throw pieces of broken wire at the wasp, until it becomes so angry that it aims its stinger at you and dives...

 Avoid getting stung
ON PAGE 30.

11
That's not right. There are 11 blue viruses that haven't been uploaded.
GO BACK TO PAGE 36 AND USE THE KEY TO HELP YOU.

68
Password rejected. Remember that each set of tallies represents 5.
THINK AGAIN ON PAGE 33.

GLOSSARY

ACTIVATE
To make something start working.

ANTI-VIRUS
An anti-virus program stops or reverses a virus in order to prevent it from harming a computer or network.

BAR CHART
A chart that shows data in bars. Each bar represents a different amount.

COMMON
In mathematics, the most common on a graph or chart is the highest amount; the least common is the lowest amount.

DATA
A set of results, scores or numerical information.

DESTROY
To damage something so much that it no longer exists.

FREQUENCY CHART
A chart that shows options and how often each option happens or is chosen.

KEY
In maths, graphs and charts can have a key to show what the symbols used mean.

LINE GRAPH
A graph that shows the relationship between two things as a line. The two data variables are set by the x-axis (horizontal) and y-axis (vertical).

MEAN
The mean is an average amount. It is calculated by adding all the totals and dividing by the number of categories.

MALFUNCTION
A fault in the way a machine should work.

MULTIPLY
To do a calculation where you add a number to itself a particular number of times.

PIE CHART
A circle that is divided into sections, each representing a proportion of the total data.

POPULAR
If something is popular it happens a lot. In maths, the most popular category in a graph or chart is the most liked or successful.

TALLY MARKS
Marks used to record a score or count an amount. Each fifth mark crosses through the four marks before, so the marks sit in sets of 5.

NETWORK
A network of computers is a group of computers that work together.

PICTOGRAM
A mathematical drawing that shows data as symbols, with a key.

VARIABLE
Something measurable that can change.

VIRUS

A program that attacks a computer or network of computers.

X-AXIS

The line marked with numbers that goes from left to right (horizontally) on a graph.

Y-AXIS

The line marked with numbers that goes from top to bottom (vertically) on a graph.

TAKING IT FURTHER

The Maths Quest books are designed to motivate children to develop and apply their maths skills through engaging adventure stories. The stories work as games in which children must solve a series of mathematical problems to progress towards the exciting conclusion.

The books do not follow a conventional pattern. The reader is directed to jump forwards and backwards through the book according to the answers given. If their answers are correct, they progress to the next part of the story; if the answer is incorrect, the reader is directed back to try the problem again. Additional support is found in the glossary.

TO SUPPORT YOUR CHILD'S MATHEMATICAL DEVELOPMENT YOU CAN:

- Read the book with your child.

- Solve the initial problems and discover how the book works.

- Continue reading with your child until he or she is using the book confidently, following the GO TO instructions to find the next puzzle or explanation.

- Encourage your child to read on alone. Ask 'What's happening now?'. Prompt your child to tell you how the story develops and what problems they have solved.

- Discuss statistics in everyday contexts: ask your child to keep a tally of all the different-coloured cars on a journey, or choose something around your house, such as windows or doors.

- Have fun with statistics calculations. Give your child six numbers – such as children's ages, items of shopping or game scores – and ask them to calculate the average (mean) by adding up the numbers and dividing by the amount (six in this case).

- Use objects or toys to make frequency charts together.

- Most of all, make maths fun!